Draw something cool

mahdi jafarian

Published by mahdi jafarian, 2024.

LEARN HOW TO DRAW EVERYTHING IN NO TIME

From simple line to advanced drawing

Mahdi Jafarian

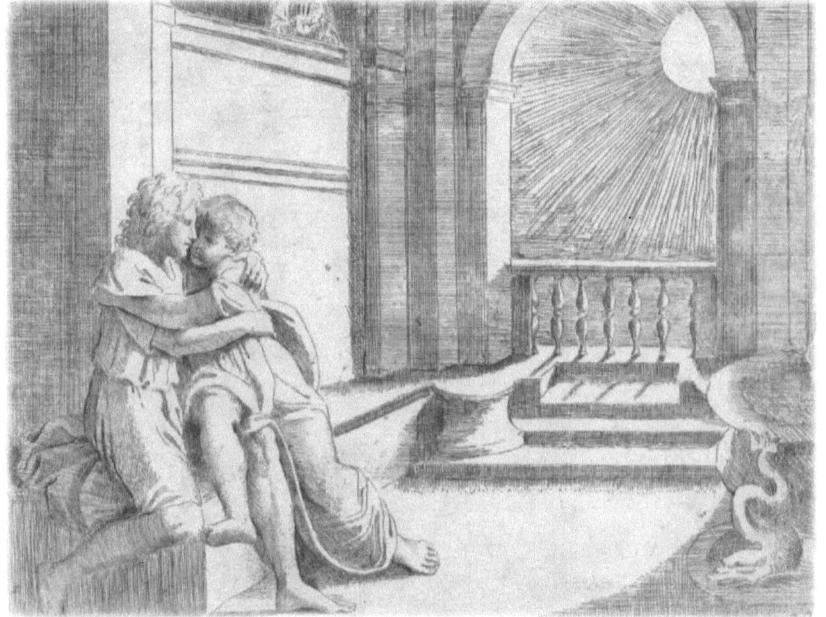

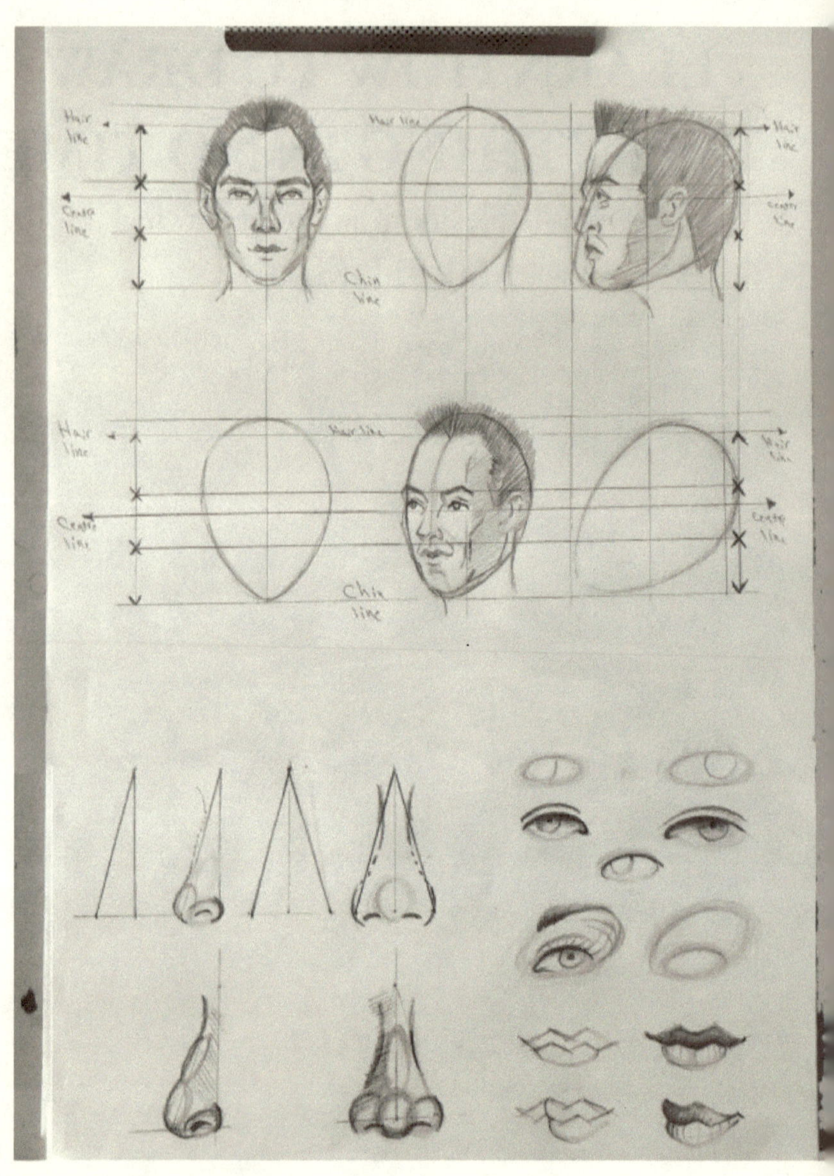

Copyright

ISBN 9798230457152

DRAW SOMETHING COOL

First edition. November 28, 2024.

ISBN: 979-8230457152

Written by mahdi jafarian.

FOREWORD

With knowledge and true understanding comes self-confidence which plays a key role in drawing. It is undeniable that learning and practising effective methods helps to achieve perfection, however having a good foundation is the key. No matter how tall and impressive a building is, faulty foundations will cause its downfall. One of the main elements in the foundation of drawing is line. For an artist, confidence comes with achieving good quality lines in drawing. If you practice consistently, it will not take long to improve your line quality and boost your confidence.

This book provides all you need to build a strong drawing foundation. You will learn drawing methods to help you achieve success in your drawing and art. Once you realise this and you have a better understanding of drawing techniques, you will be surprised by your progress. As your confidence grows, you will overcome many of the obstacles that confront many artists.

If you are looking for a quick, easy way to improve your drawing skills, this is the book for you. It will save you a lot of time in your quest to be a better artist.

Table of contents:

Introduction

Often artists focus on a single subject. For some it is nature, others prefer to draw portraits. However professional artists achieve a high standard in their work, regardless of the subject.

Professional artists share one key quality, the ability to use their imagination to achieve better and quicker results. For example, when an artist is drawing a live portrait, time may be limited. If the subject cannot sit still, the task is even more challenging. The artist's priority is to capture the general form of the sitter quickly and then use imagination and memory to complete the portrait. It is still possible for the artist to make changes, to improve the work or please the sitter.

Let me explain this use of the imagination. All artists unconsciously create a library of shapes in their mind. This process takes place as they develop their drawing skills. The more they draw from their imagination, the more they use this library in their mind, where, for example, they might have different shapes of lips. When drawing a portrait, the artist can call on the store of shapes in his imagination to draw the lips of even the most restless sitter.

Now you can understand why it is important to start from a good foundation from the start. Some people have not mastered the skill of drawing shapes correctly after many years of trying. They often find it difficult to improve their technique because they have been repeating the same errors in their technique for all those years. They attribute their poor drawing ability to a lack of talent. What they lack, in fact, is a solid foundation for their learning.

After attaining a high level of skill in drawing lines, an artist must then gain a good understanding of perspective, dimension and proportion.

Secrets of Lines

With lines you can draw anything. With practice, you can even create shading effects using lines. Initially you will notice your mistakes when you use lines for shading whereas this is not the case when you shade without lines. Mastering shading with lines means you have made significant progress in your drawing technique.

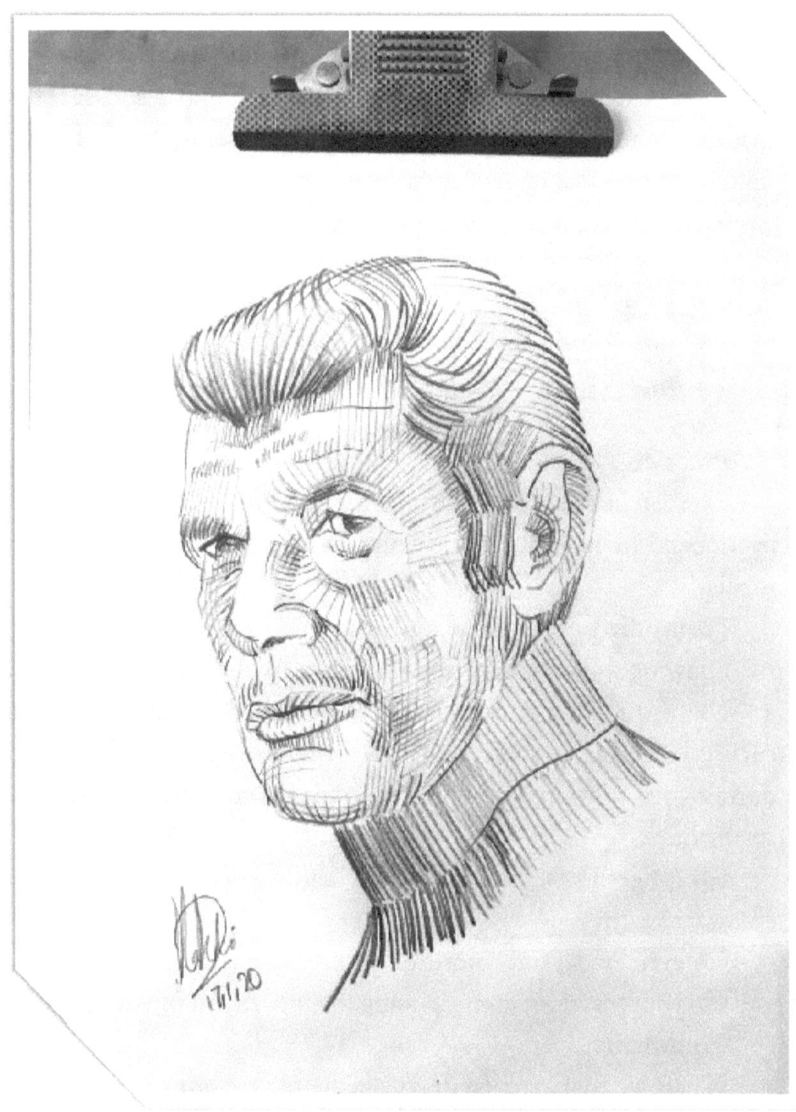

With lines you can draw anything. With practice, you can even create shading effects using lines. Initially you will notice your mistakes when you use lines for shading whereas this is not the case when you shade without lines. Mastering shading with lines means you have made significant progress in your drawing technique.

Factors affecting the quality of line drawing include:

- confidence
- positioning of the hand and arm
- practice

Practice

Consistent practice is essential for good line drawing, but it is often overlooked or neglected. You will not improve if you do not practise regularly.

Positioning of the hand and arm

Drawing short lines involves your fingers and wrist.

Use a throwing hand movement to practise drawing straight and curved lines. Vary the speed of your hand movements from fast to slow during your practice and you will gradually achieve fluency and firm, strong lines.

For longer lines, lock your finger and wrist to use the joint of your elbow correctly.

For even longer lines, position your hand and arm like a straight stick and use your shoulder joint to guide the movement of your pencil.

Confidence

When we first start to draw, our hands are not confident. Is it our hands or ourselves? If we are fearful and hesitant our lines will be faint and unsteady resulting in drawings of poor quality. Think of a boxer with the ability to punch firmly and the flexibility to adjust his speed. As his confidence grows, so does his ability. It is the same with drawing where our hands need to be firm and flexible to produce good work.

Be brave, be fearless, practise drawing different lines at different speeds. As your lines become firmer and better, you will become more adventurous.

It doesn't matter how many pages you fill during your line practice or how incompetent you feel. Focus on the fact that you are overcoming the psychological barrier to progress and becoming a fearless drawer, like a musketeer overcoming an enemy.

The more you believe in yourself while practising, the sooner your line quality will improve.

After all, everything we practise consciously goes into our subconscious. When we first started to drive a car or learn an instrument, it was tricky but after a while we could do it subconsciously. Sometimes we don't even remember the details of a twenty-minute drive home.

Your aim is to become a fluent drawer so that you can draw everything quickly and create a lot of detail in a short space of time. When you reach this stage, you will be surprised at how much cross hatching and shading you can complete so quickly. Your subconscious takes control where there is repetition. This enables you to save energy for creativity (conciously) on the less repetitive and more challenging aspects of the drawing.

The way our subconcious works explains why the more you practice drawing, the better you become.

Practising Lines:

You will need a drawing pencil (You can start with a HB pencil and later try any sort of pencil to challenge yourself), a sketch board, several A2, A3, A4 sheets of paper, a ruler.

1. Place an A3 sheet of paper on your sketch board and start drawing parallel straight lines from left to right, right to left, then up and down, down and up.

Draw diagonal lines in both directions.

Practice will strengthen your hand to draw the lines in the direction you find the most difficult.

Draw longer parallel lines as close to each other as you can. Repeat the steps and draw curved lines.

Now try circles and draw inner and outer circles and do the same for ovals and any other curved shape you like. Repeat this process for at least three days.

Next, using A2 paper, repeat the process. Your lines will be longer, your shapes bigger. Try even larger sheets of paper if you can. Keep switching your practice from big to small and vice versa.

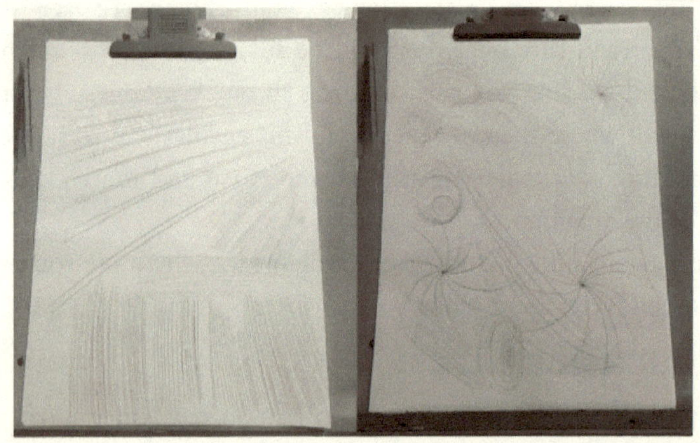

2. Draw dots at various places on your sheet of paper and connect these dots with good quality, firm lines. Start with short distances and, once you improve, increase the distance gradually.

Repeat the activity using curved lines.

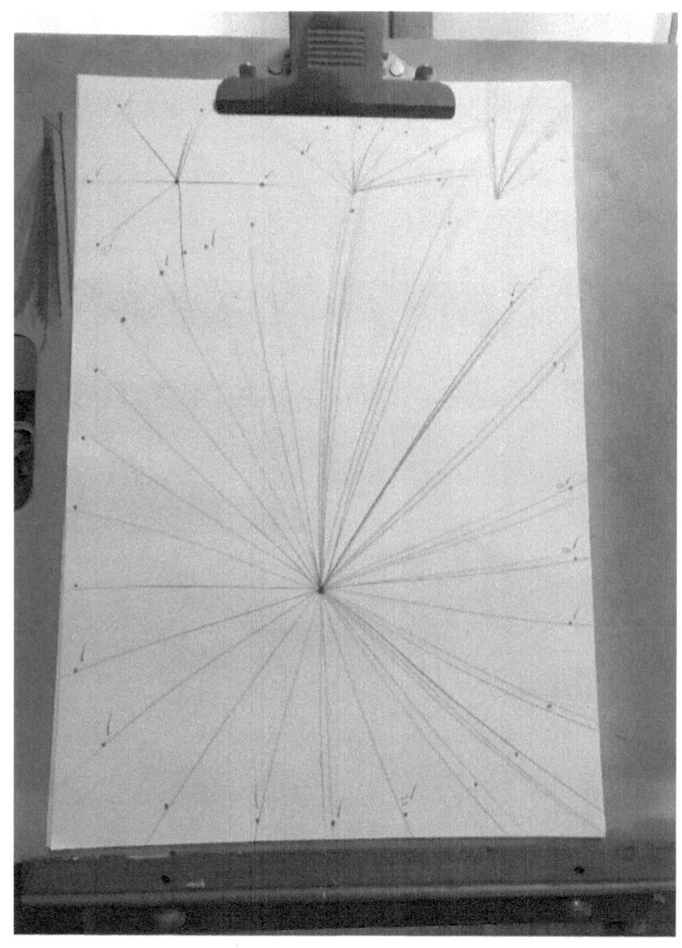

1. Draw horizontal straight lines, 2 cm in length, without using your ruler or any other measuring tool. Draw several lines and then measure them to gauge your accuracy.

Repeat the activity with vertical and diagonal lines.

Repeat the activity with lines of different lengths.

This exercise trains your hands, eyes and brain to gauge proportions accurately and enables you to draw horizonal, vertical and diagonal lines of the same length quickly and easily.

Repeat the process using curved lines.

This exercise will make it easier for you to divide lines into equal parts as required.

Be creative and practise in different ways such as drawing a hexagon.

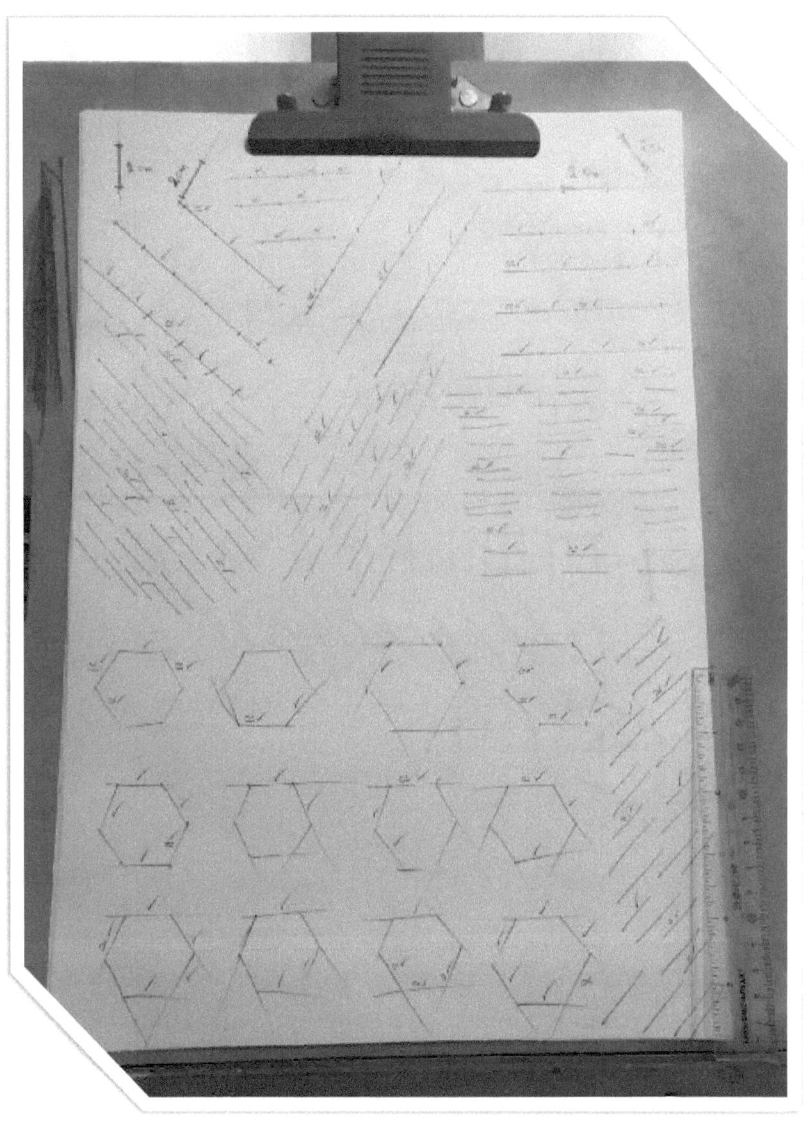

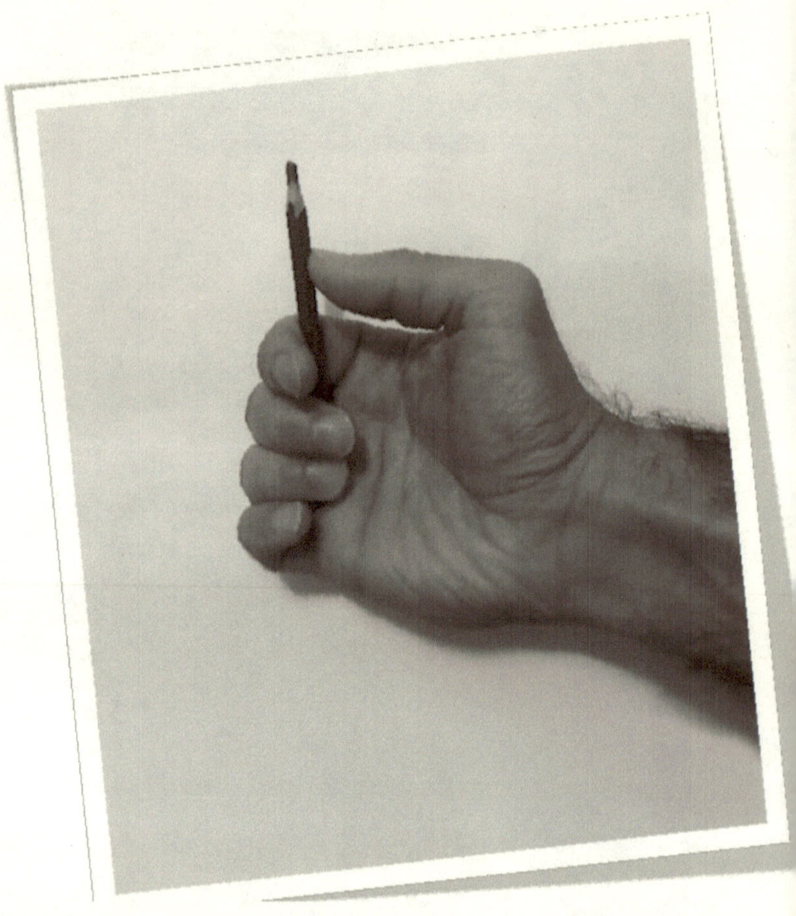

Once you are good at this, you will find it easy to use the technique of measuring angles and proportions by holding a pencil straight out in front of you. This is a well-known technique which is explained in detail on many websites and in several books. Some people have no success with this famous technique because they have not mastered the ability to judge lengths and angles without measuring them.

1. Experiment with your pencil grip during your drawing practice. Although this can be challenging at first, you will come to appreciate the different effects this will have on your

lines. Try all the variations that come to mind. Don't give up on the difficult methods. Try to make it fun and work out how the different methods come in handy for different tasks. Different pencils can help you to achieve different textures and tonality. The degree of pressure you apply to the pencil is also a key factor in producing the effect you want.

Once you are good with lines, the next step is to apply them to your drawings as contour lines to create shapes. Try to look at as many drawings done with contour lines as you can. There is no limit to the effects and textures that can be achieved with contour lines. Also take notice of the correct angles, directions and thickness of the contour lines applied in great drawings.

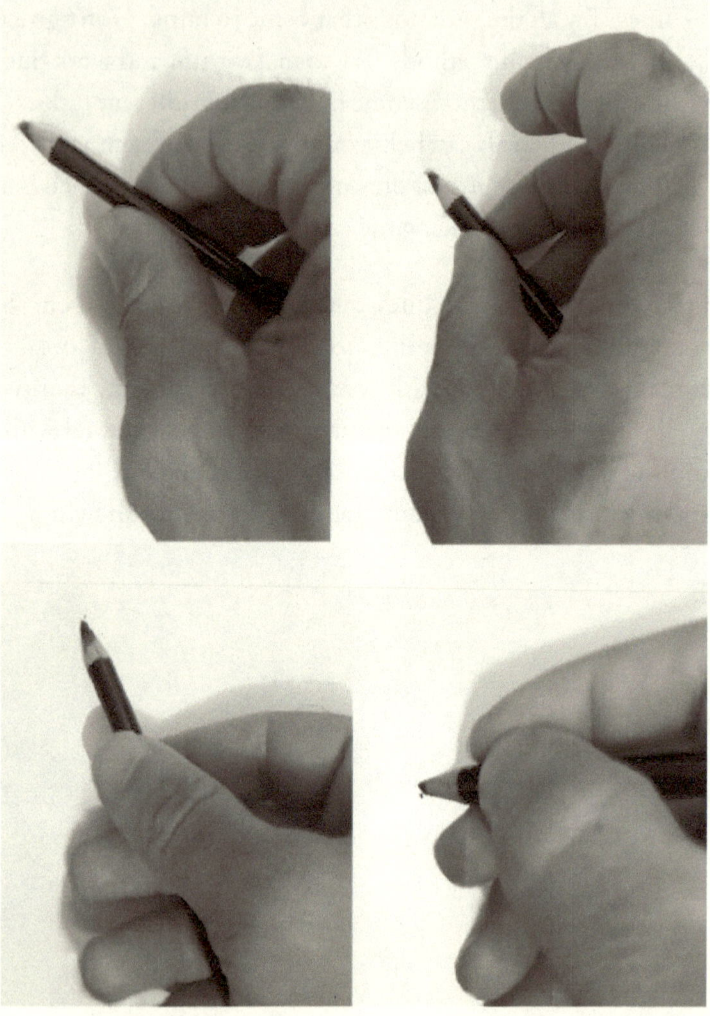

1. You should always pay attention to the tip of your pencil when drawing. With time you will be able to recognize which side and angle of your pencil tip is the best for the line effect you want to achieve. Eventually you will become so familiar with the state of your pencil tip that you will get the best out of it even when it is not in great shape.

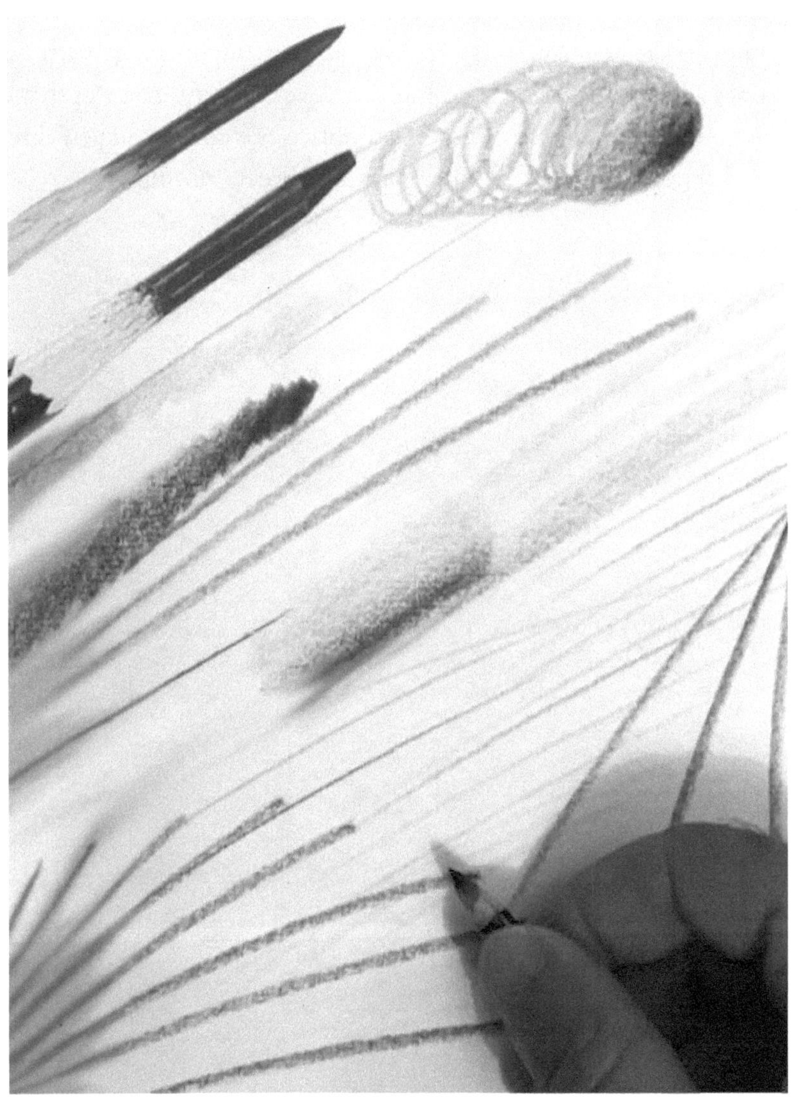

Once you are confident with drawing lines, start using them as contour lines to create shapes. Try to look at as many drawings with contour lines as possible. There is no limit to the effects and textures that can be achieved with contour lines. Also notice the correct angles, directions and thickness of contour lines applied in great drawings.

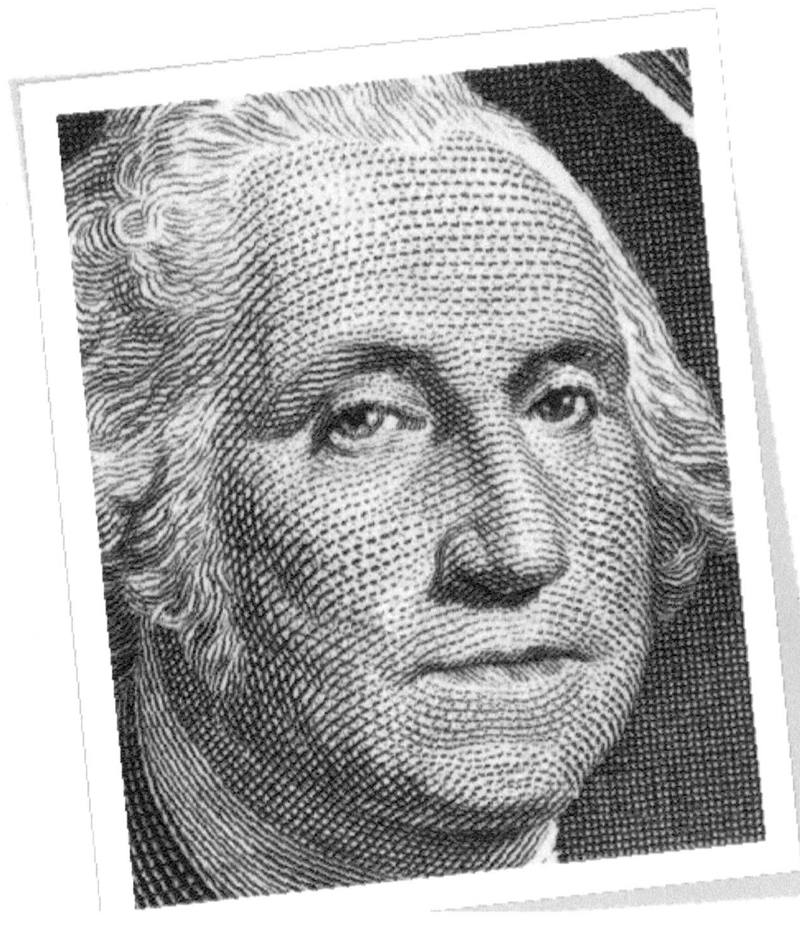

1. I really recommend you do all the above practices with your other hand too. It is a big challenge for your brain and once you switch to your dominant hand again you will appreciate how much easier it is. Try not to forget to use your other hand more often after this. This will bring you huge progress in the long term.

Unique Practices that Unlock the Brain's Potential to Draw

Here are some important facts about our brains that we can use to improve our drawing and achieve great results.

The left side of our brain controls the right side of our body and the right side of our brain controls the left side of our body. When we cross our hands or feet, we cross the imaginary midline of our body and engage both sides of our brain.

At our sketch boards when we draw long lines from one side of a large sheet of paper to the other, we cross the midline of our body with our hand and arm.

It is important to know that the right side of the brain is associated with creativity and art as well as emotion and intuition while the left side deals with logic as in science and mathematics. This explains why right-brained people who are left-handed are often good at art and creativity. Leonardo da Vinci, for example, was left-handed.

After attaining a high level of skill in drawing lines, an artist must then gain a good understanding of perspective, dimension and proportion. Although art and creativity relate to the right side of the brain, perspective, dimension and proportion relate to the left side of the brain. It doesn't matter if you are right-handed or left-handed, the more you practise the correct techniques, the higher the standard you will achieve.

Practice

You will need the same equipment as before plus an extra pencil and an easel.

1. Using your non-dominant hand, repeat all the practice exercises listed earlier under The Secrets of Lines.

1. Set up a sketch board on an easel.

Stand in front of the easel and with your pencil, start practising lines and drawings.

Change your position every five or ten minutes from left to right then right to left of the easel.

In each position, try to draw with each hand for at least 5 minutes.

Continue to change your hand and position as you wish to challenge yourself.

1. After a while when you feel quite confident using your non-dominant hand, take a pencil in each hand and practise drawing lines with both hands.

Try to do a drawing with both hands. Start with a simple drawing and gradually make it more challenging as you make progress.

While you are drawing, remember to cross your hands some of the time so you get used to it.

1. Set up an easel on a sketch board and position yourself in front of the easel with your back to a model. Whether you choose an object, or a live model depends on how much you want to challenge yourself.

Turn and look at the model every few seconds as you draw the image on the sketch board.

This will greatly increase your photographic memory.

Once you feel confident with this, try it with your non-dominant hand.

1. Try to draw your models from different angles and heights. Sometimes position yourself higher than the model, sometimes lower even when you are drawing live portraits.

This way you will get used to foreshortening and optical illusion in drawing. If you don't have access to a live model, try using a statue or a bust.

1. Set up a model behind a sketch board.

Now stand in front of the sketch board and try drawing the model without looking at the sketch board at all.

Imagine that your pencil is moving on the model, touching it and don't lift your pencil from the paper at all. The lines on the paper will show how you have been moving your pencil from one part of the model to another.

You will be surprised how poor your drawing is at first but how good it becomes with practice.

Later you will appreciate how much quicker and more efficient you become when you have the freedom to look at the model and the sketch board with no restrictions.

This practice will make it easier for you to do normal drawings and to connect better with your model.

1. When you are doing your daily tasks use your non-dominant hand some of the time to challenge your brain and unlock its potential. For example, when you are eating, use your non-dominant hand to hold the cutlery.

If you think about it there are many ways to unlock the potential of your brain. Try holding your pencil with your toes sometimes during your drawing practice sessions. As you know there are many people with disabilities who are great artists and who have no choice but to use their toes to draw.

By the time you complete all the practice exercises, you should be a fearless drawer. In the past negative feedback might have discouraged you from drawing. Not now! You have gained enough confidence and you are improving day by day, so now you don't care what other people think.

Don't be afraid of making mistakes, embrace them. Recognising your mistakes is a sign of progress

Methods to become a Fluent Drawer

1. Relax your arm so it is less stiff, more dynamic. Stiffness is completely different to firmness. Firm lines create a great drawing.

Warm up by practising straight and curved lines before you start the main drawing.

When you are a beginner you might find it easier to draw a few shorter, firm lines instead of drawing one long line.

Create a good composition by drawing the bigger shapes using soft lines first.

Don't focus on details at this point.

Use basic shapes to define the placement of the elements of the drawing.

Add thickness where lines bend or connect to each other.

Draw with faster, more dynamic strokes.

1. In your drawing try to draw the main gesture first. (Gesture is the pose, form or action of the subject you are drawing).

Initially, create stability and structure with a few main strokes.

Now work around that stable gesture to create movement with strokes representing energy.

There should always be energy in your drawing even if the subject is still.

1. Simplify the drawing using basic shapes for the subject and the background.

Start with faint lines to establish the structure and placement of different elements.

Gradually use darker, firmer lines to create the drawing.

Leave the details until last.

1. Remember that gesture, proportion, perspective and composition must be established before you start shading or colouring your drawing.

Use some contour lines around the gesture first to establish the fundamentals of the drawing.

Add more contour lines or a mixture of contour lines and shading to complete your drawing. The choice depends on which technique you prefer.

1. Life drawing is the best option for refining your technique, but if this is not possible, make sure that you have a good photo as a reference during your drawing.

The photo should have distinct areas of light and shade as well as good perspective and composition.

The drawings of old masters are a good place to start. You will learn a lot from their works.

1. Don't outline your drawings. Look at the drawings of the old masters. You rarely see an outline in their compositions.

Lines are acceptable, however, to separate surfaces or define a shape, shade or shadow.

1. There is a technique that I call 'the stormy sketch'. It takes one to two minutes. It's very messy but quick.

The secret is not to lift your pencil off the paper during the two minutes. Draw very quickly most of the time but adjust your speed intermittently.

I recommend that you add this to your regular practice exercises.

Press lightly on the pencil most of the time so that you can establish the gesture and composition of your drawing in faint lines.

After two minutes of stormy sketching, you can work on your drawing using stronger and firmer lines.

You will be amazed how accurate your speedy, stormy sketch will be.

Try it! It will boost your confidence.

I usually do a stormy sketch just before I start a twenty to sixty minutes live portrait.

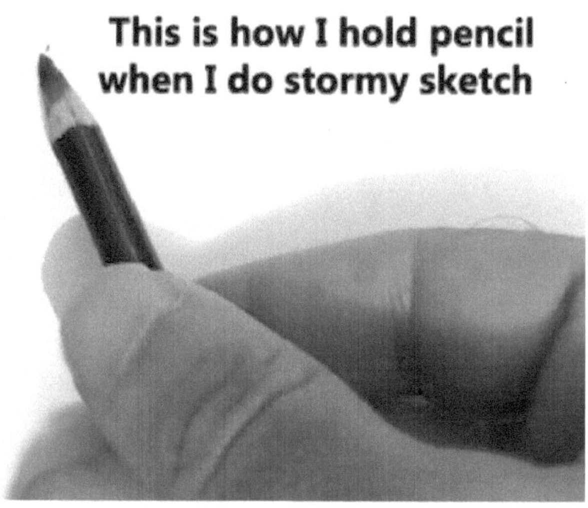

Some samples of my stormy sketches done in under two minutes

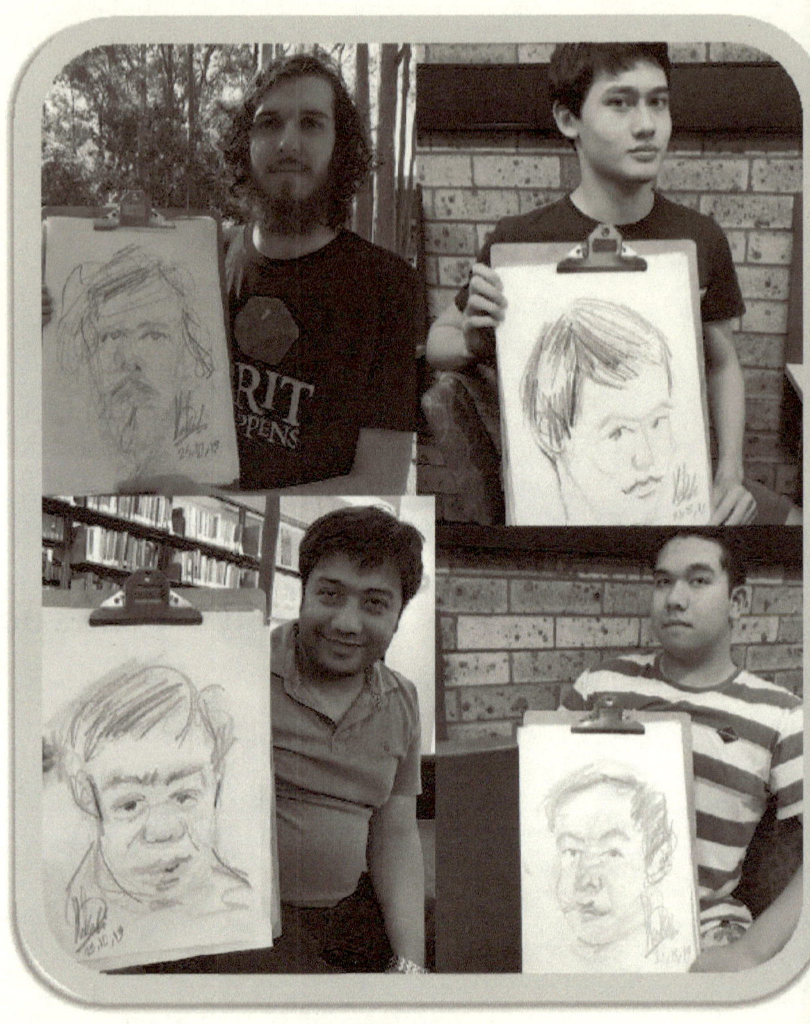

Here are some photos of portraits I have done in twenty minutes (I believe that portraits done in under an hour are more artistic and fun to look at)

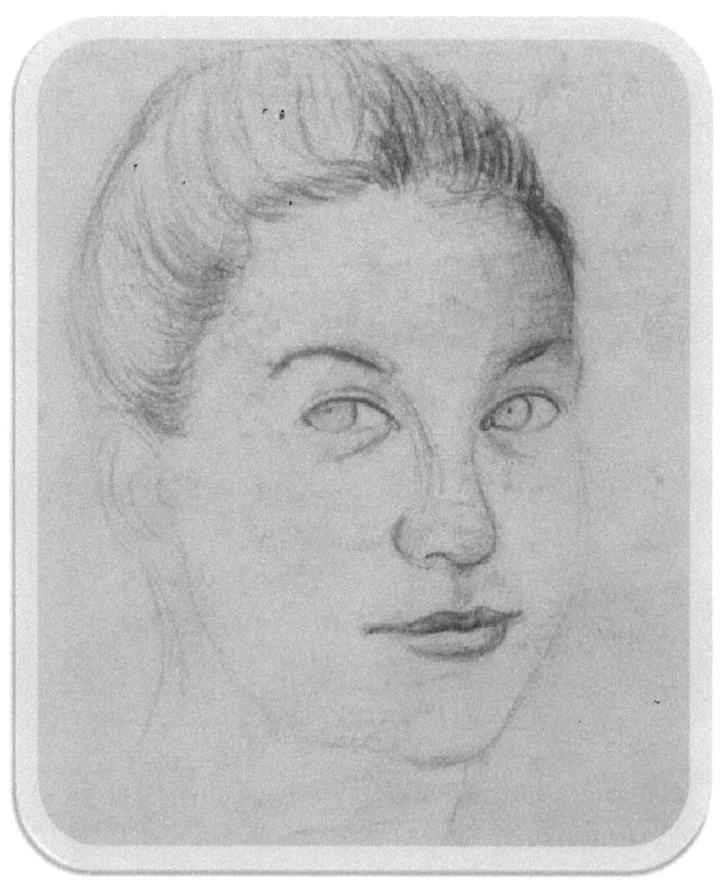

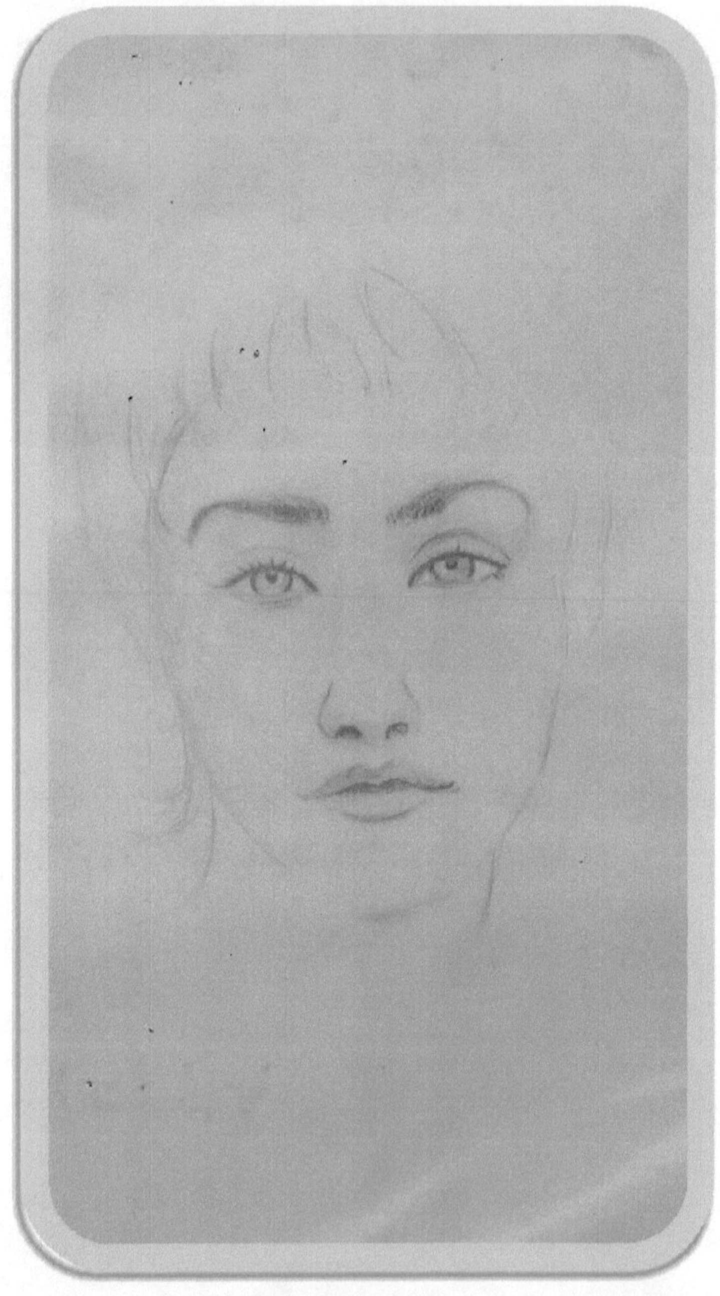

Sometimes you can use photos to practise drawing faces.

Don't force yourself to achieve an exact likeness at first. Give free rein to your creative potential so you can have more fun and draw more easily and fluently.

This can help you develop more belief in yourself as an artist. You will find it easier to achieve the exact likeness later. Once you build your self-confidence through drawing practice, you will feel the real power of your creativity.

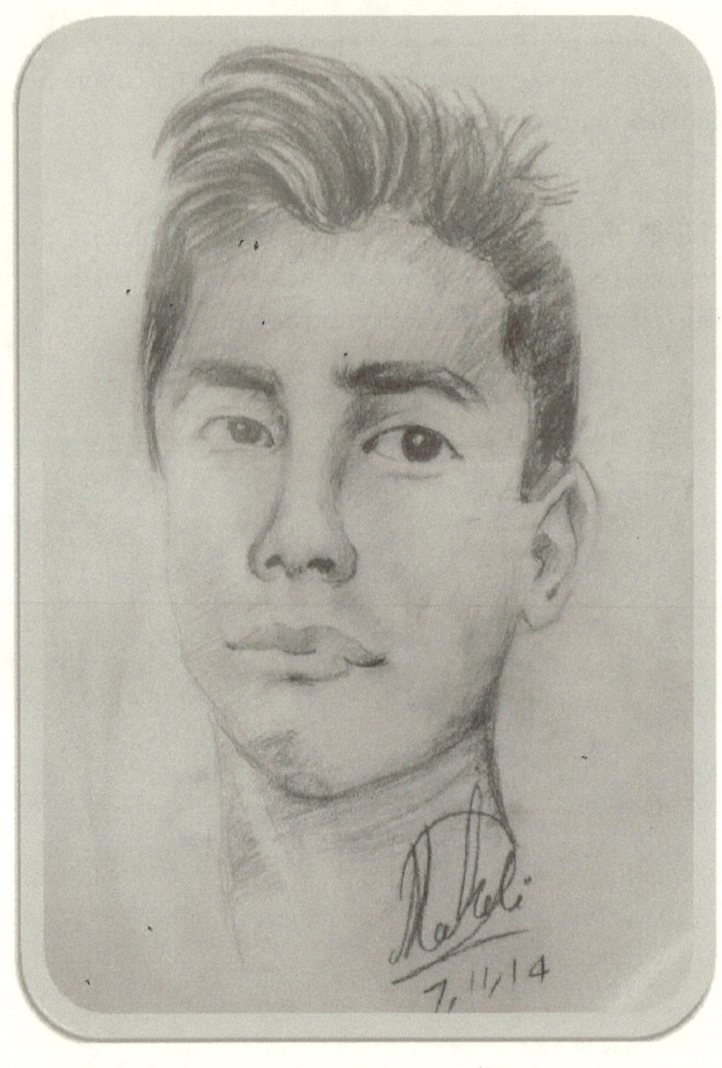
7/11/14

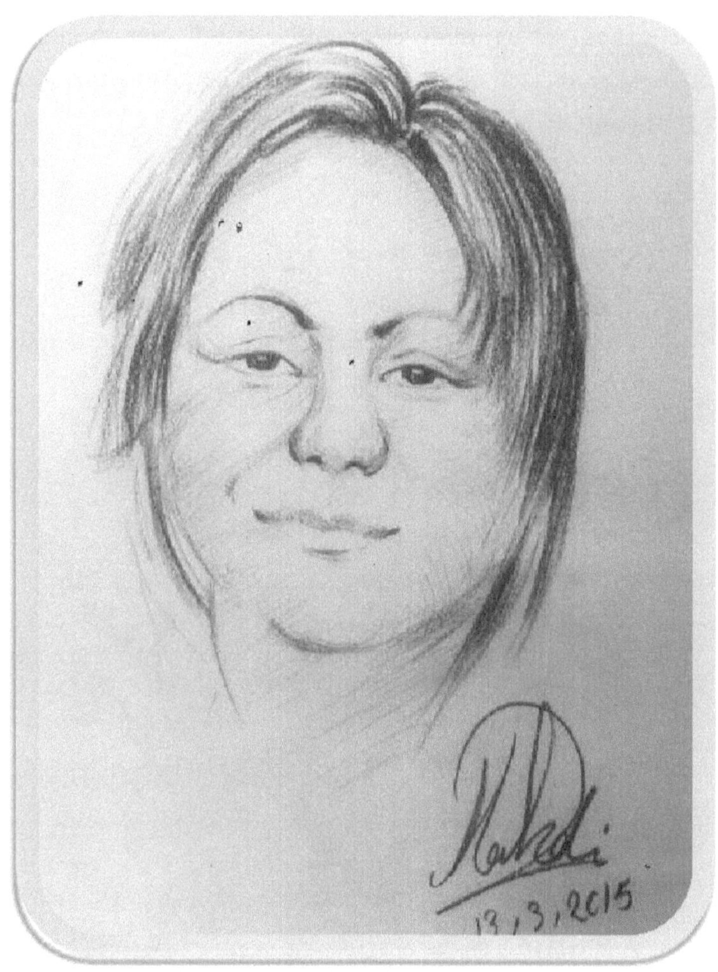

If there is not enough time, don't push yourself to draw every detail of the face. Use quick hatching on the side where there is more shade if you don't have time to draw contour lines. Try to close your left eye some of the time when you are looking at a live model. This is a quick way to change your view from 3D to 2D. If you didn't have a chance to do much at all, it doesn't matter. Ask the model if you can take a photo. Later use the photo to analyse the face more closely and to work on the portrait. You will notice many details that you missed during the sitting.

Some sitters are naturally calm and relaxed. You should always remember to be relaxed while drawing live portraits as the sitter will follow your example.

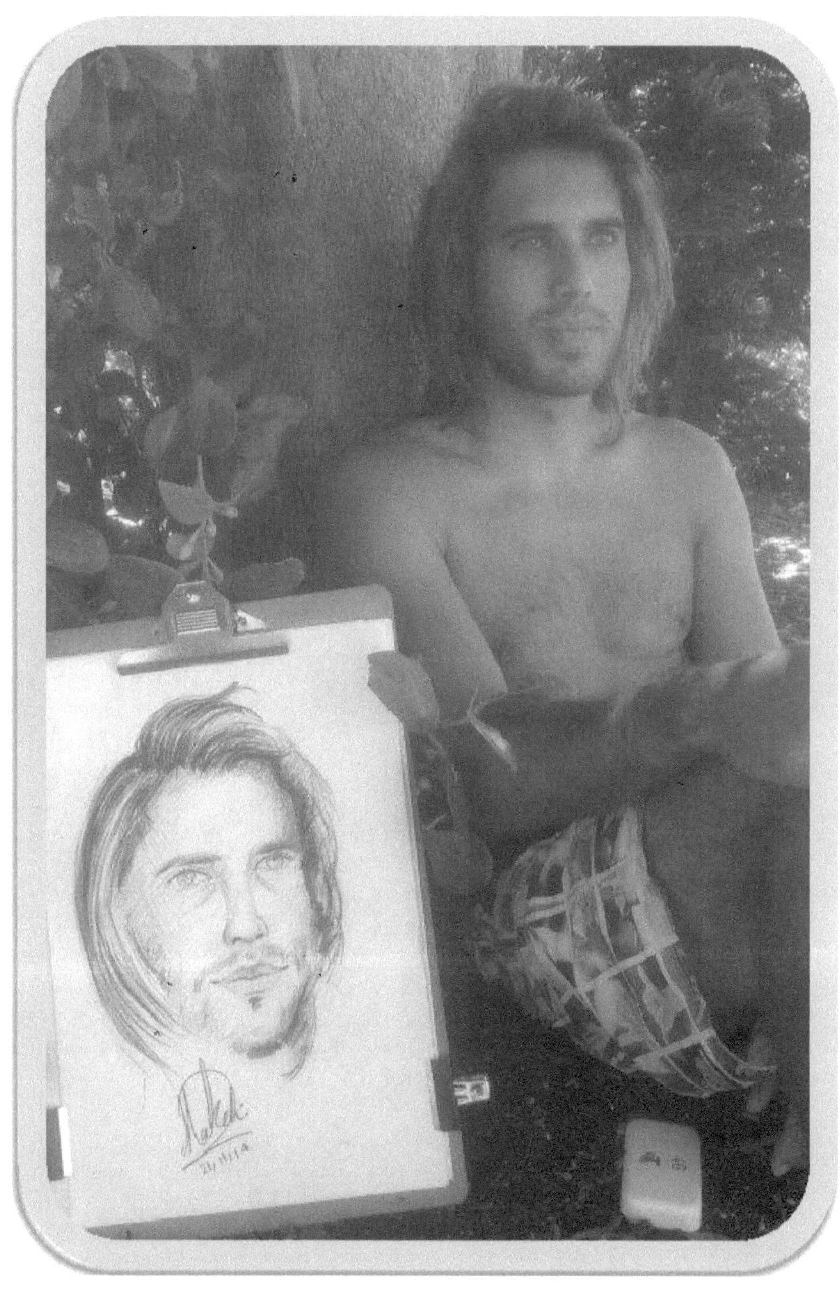

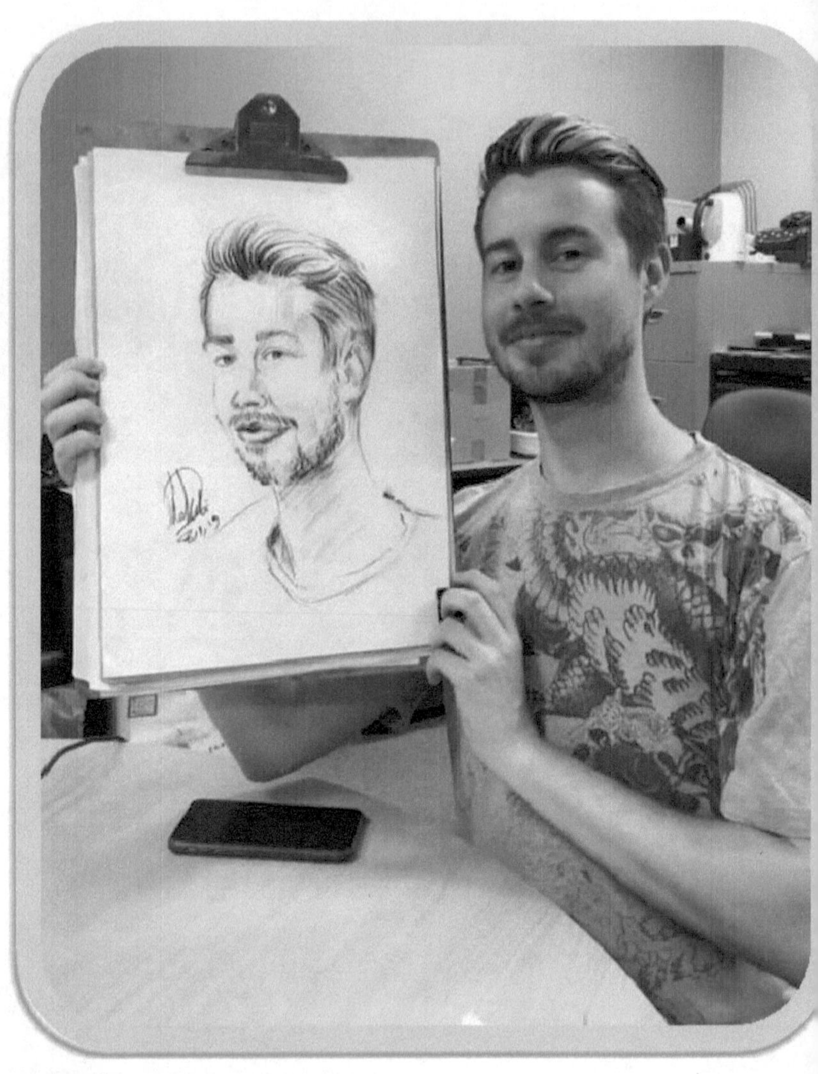

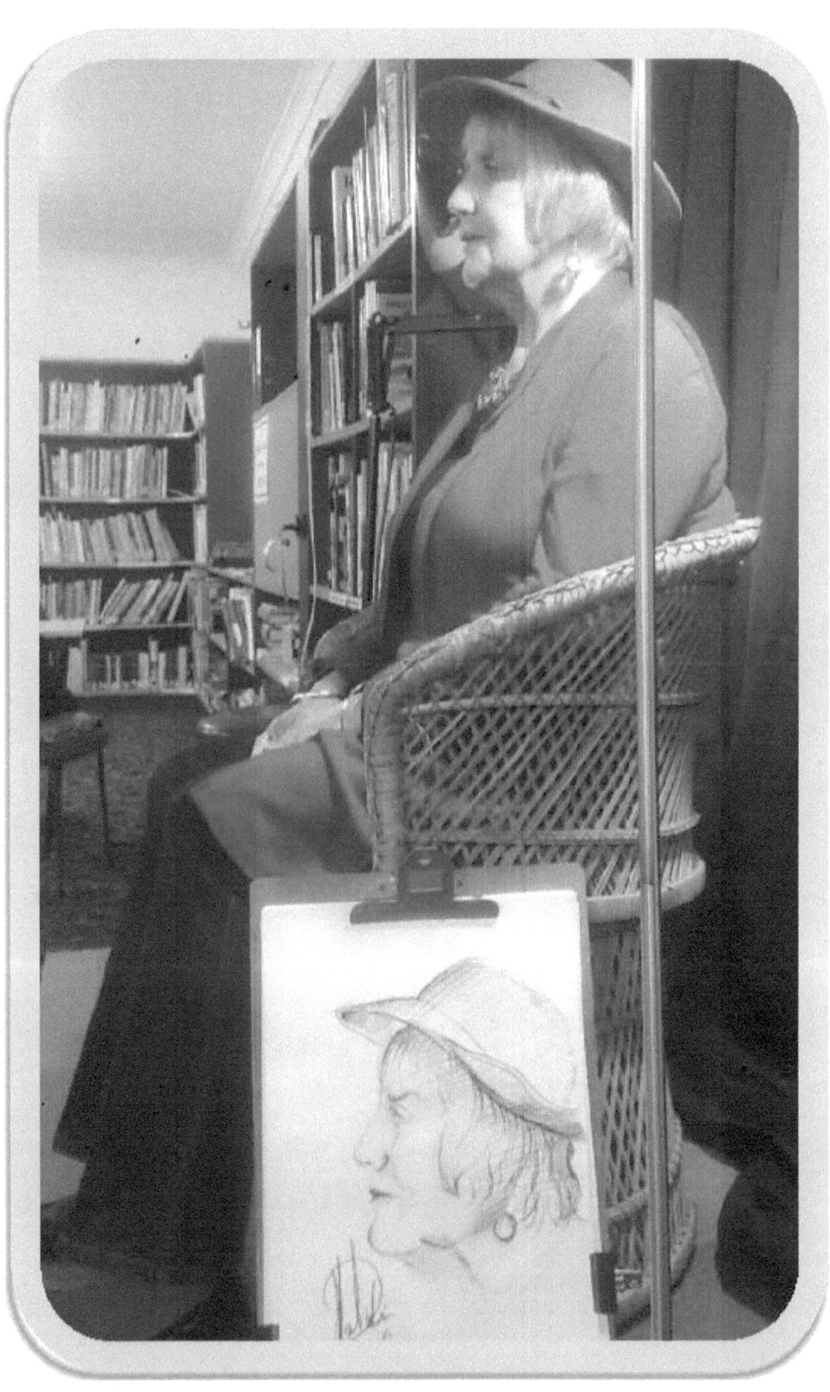

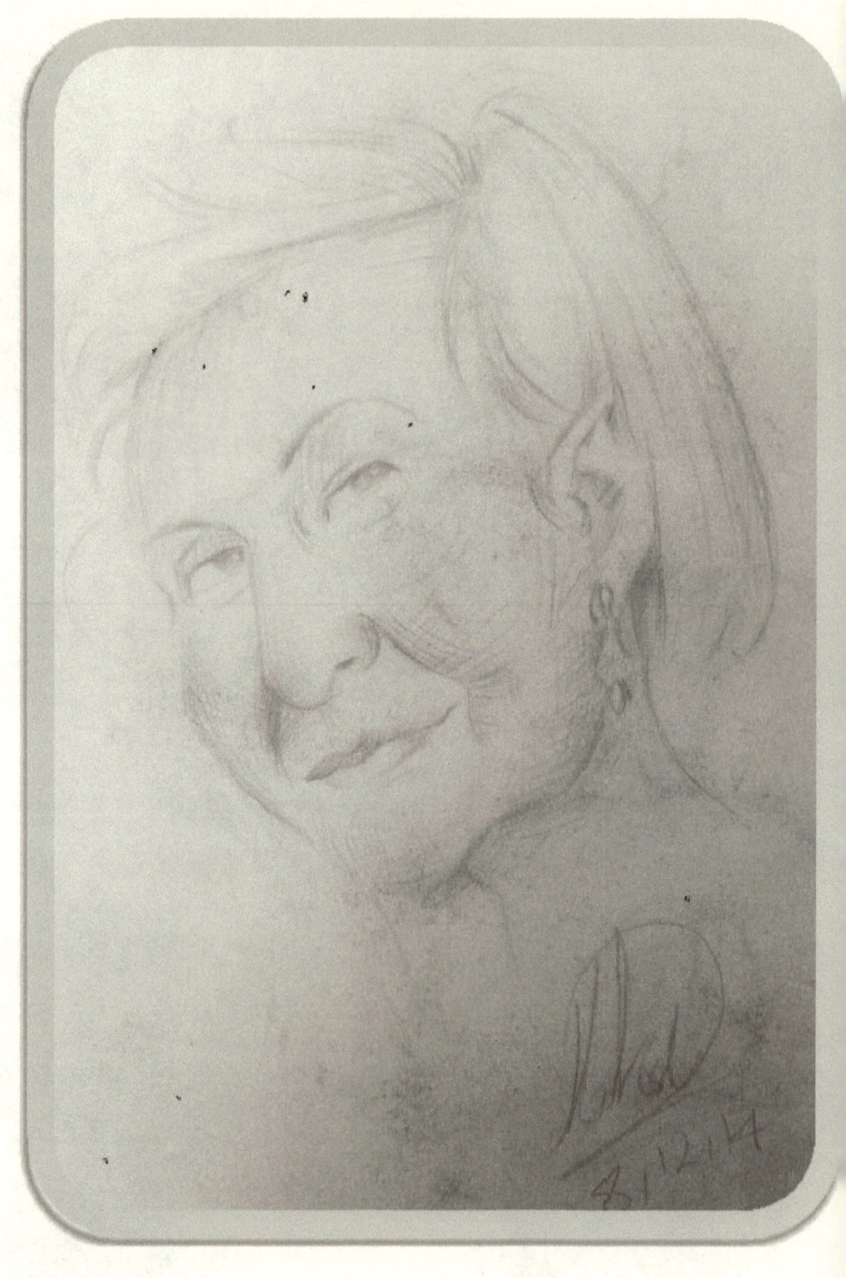

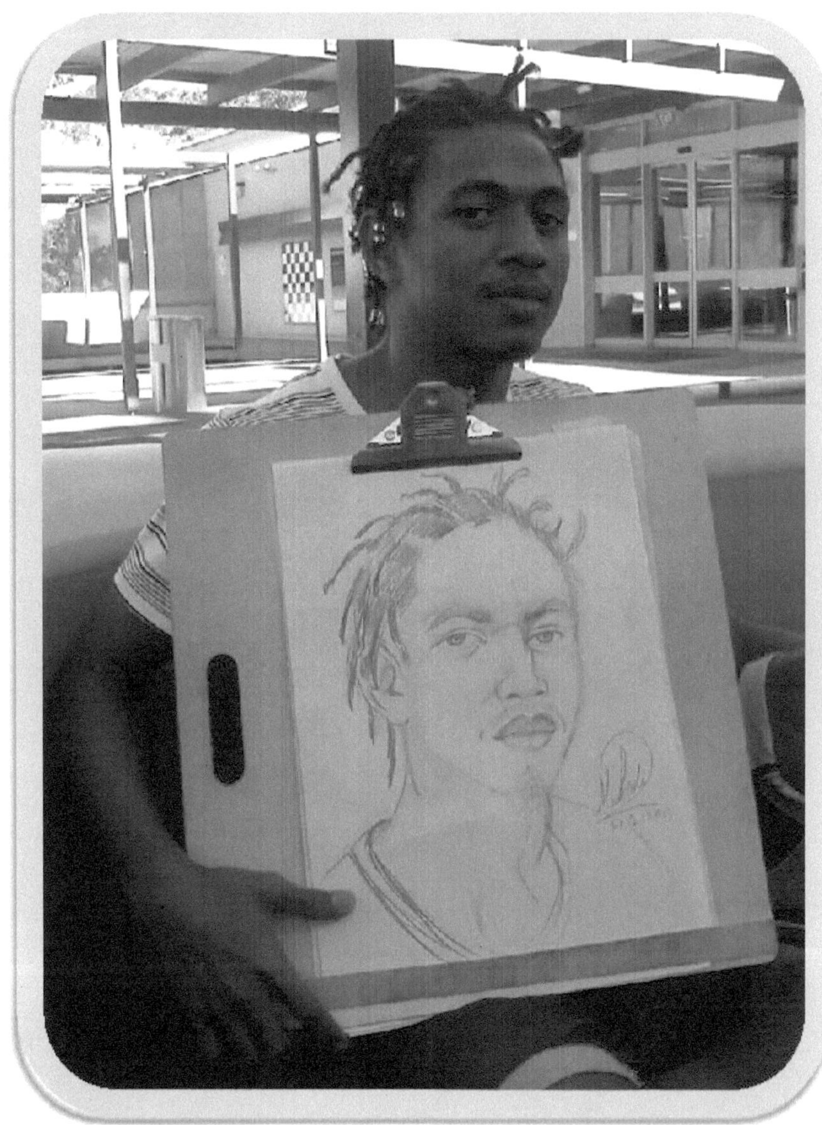

On many occasions, the models look at you very seriously when you draw them, but when you want to take a picture they smile. If this is the case you will have to ask them to put on their serious face while you take their photo.

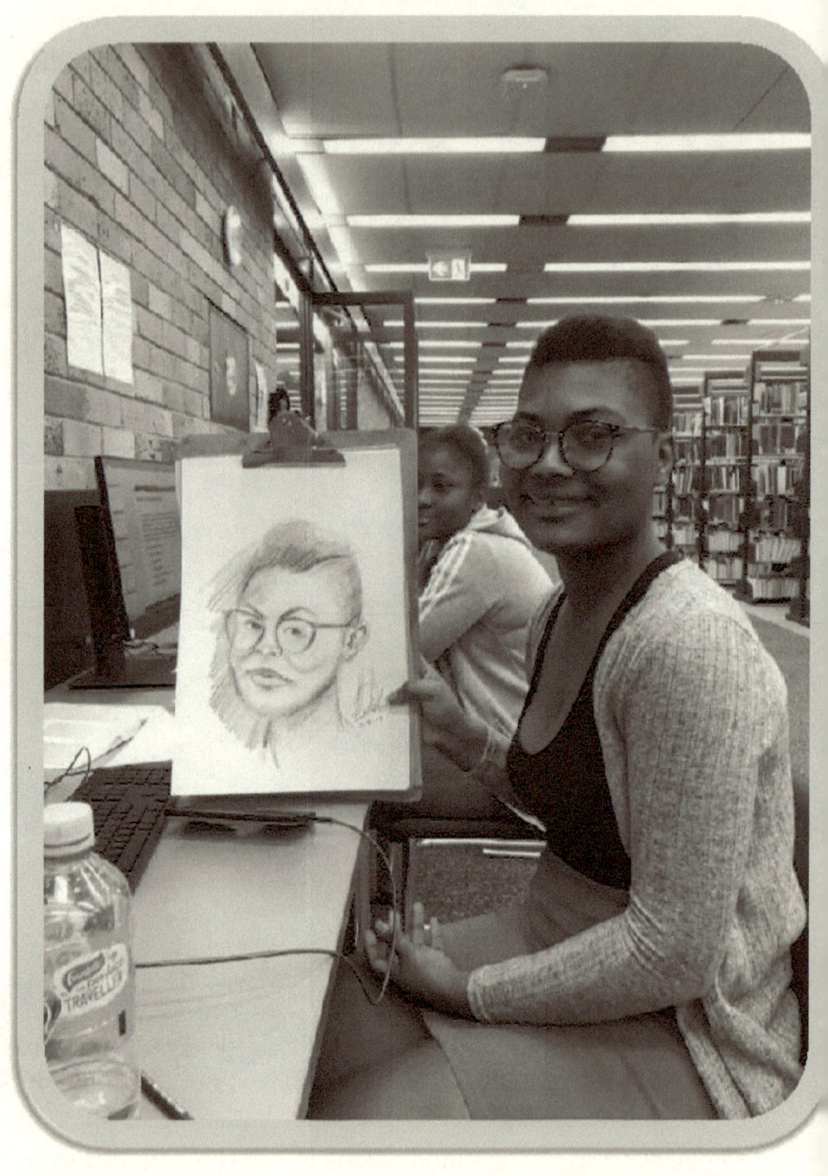

Applying perspective to your drawings

There is a lot to learn about perspective and there are lots of books which focus exclusively on perspective. Simply stated, perspective relates to vanishing point and eye level. In my reading I have found that many books overcomplicate perspective by trying to explain it without diagrams. In this book I aim to provide you with brief, practical hints to use in your drawings.

One Point Perspective

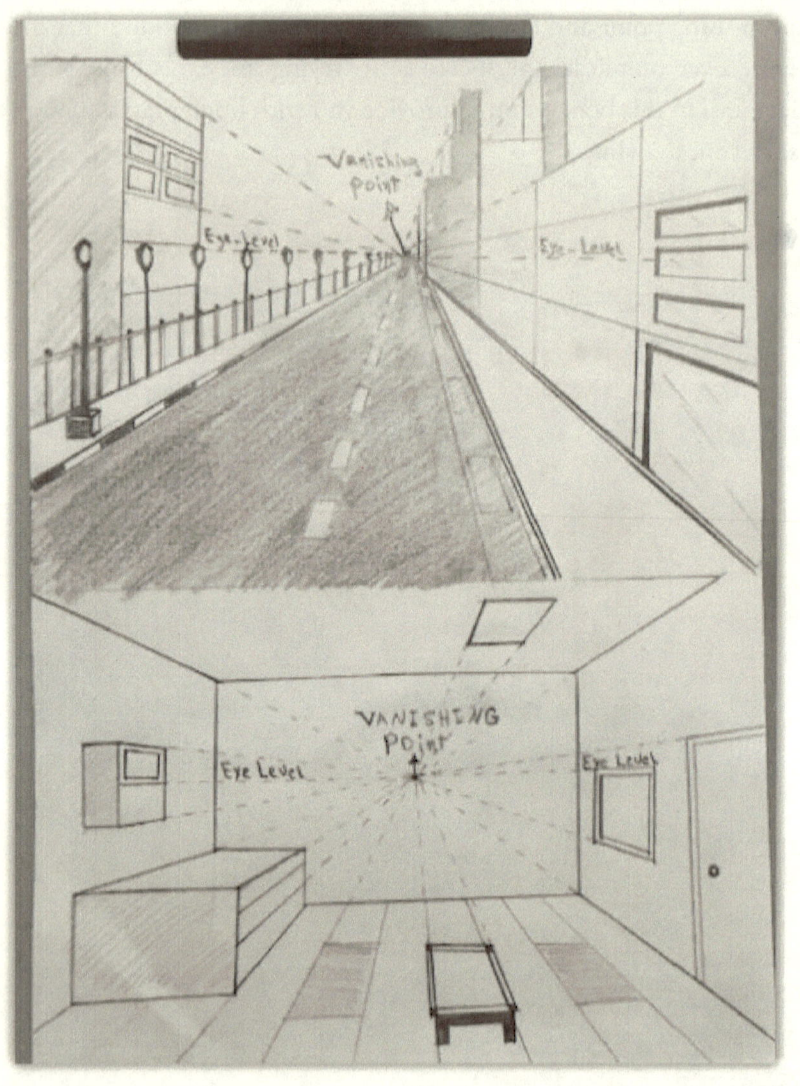

One point perspective is a method of drawing in which objects become smaller as their distance from the viewer increases, receding towards a point called the vanishing point. The vanishing point is directly in front of the viewer. It is at the viewer's eye level, an imaginary line which designates the horizon in the drawing.

Two Point Perspective

Using this technique, an artist can draw a three-dimensional object in two dimensions. As the diagram below illustrates, the parallel lines representing each dimension converge at eye level. Two point perspective is used for drawing both interior and exterior spaces.

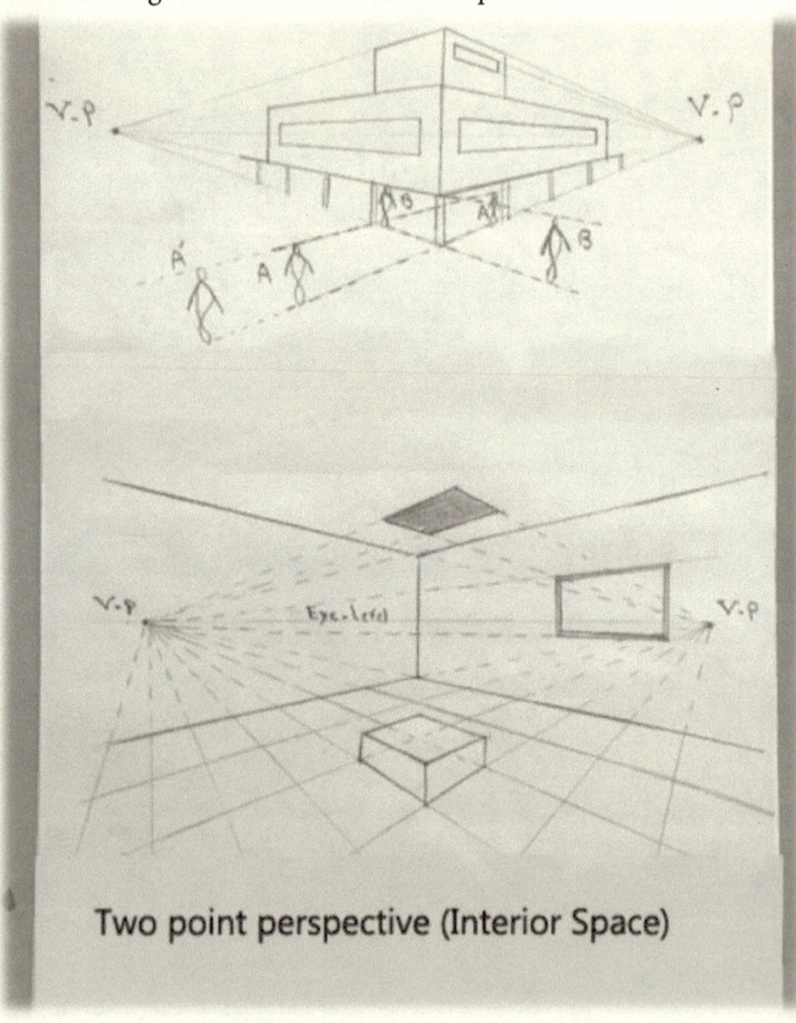

Two point perspective (Interior Space)

Look at Figures A and B and compare each one to the height of the columns. Which one is taller? By extending the base line and height line for Figures A and B, we can see that Figure A looks slightly smaller despite being closer to us. If we continue to extend the lines however, Figure A seems taller and closer.

Perspective in Portraits

It is important to consider perspective when we are drawing portraits. Many of the problems experienced by beginners relate to perspective. Although the human head is three-dimensional it can look flat in drawings where perspective has been overlooked.

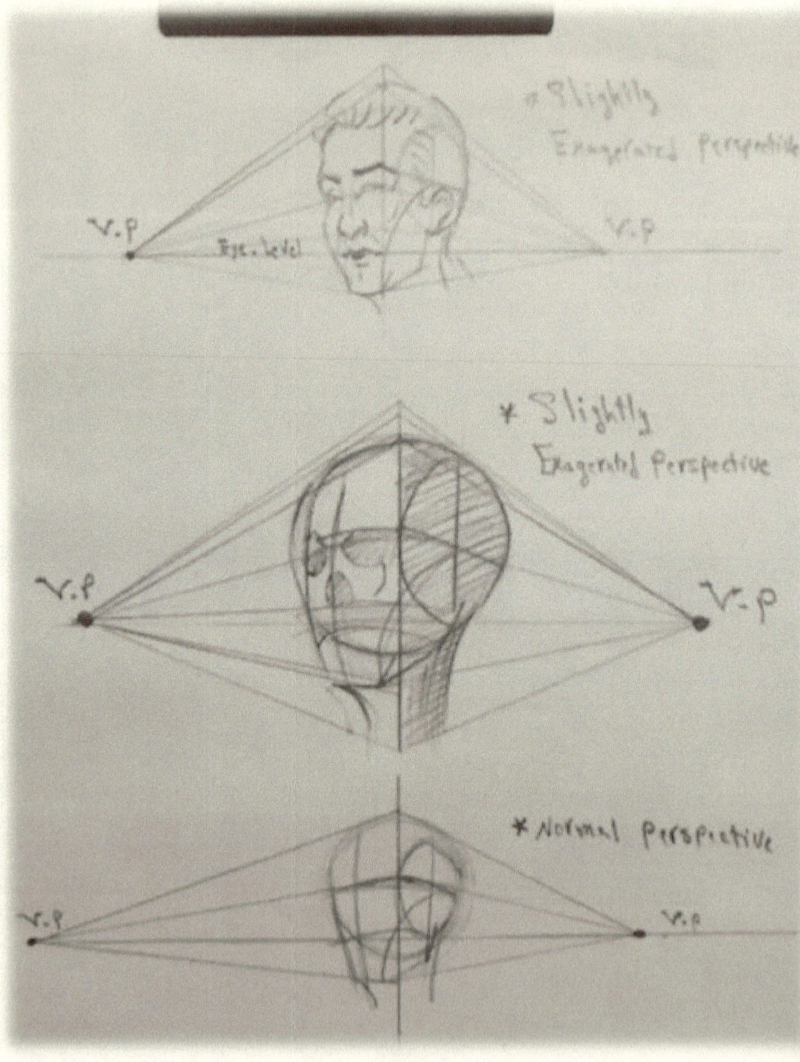

The vanishing point on the left side of the subject's face in the first two examples should be further away from the drawing.The subject's left eye needs to be slightly higher than its current position because the eyes are almost at the same level. I had to exaggerate the drawing slightly so that the vanishing point on the left side fits onto the page. See how the line goes from the centre through each eye then recedes to the vanishing point. The viewer's eyes are at the same height as the subject's lips, thus the imaginary 'eye-level' line in this drawing goes through the lips.

Three Point Perspective

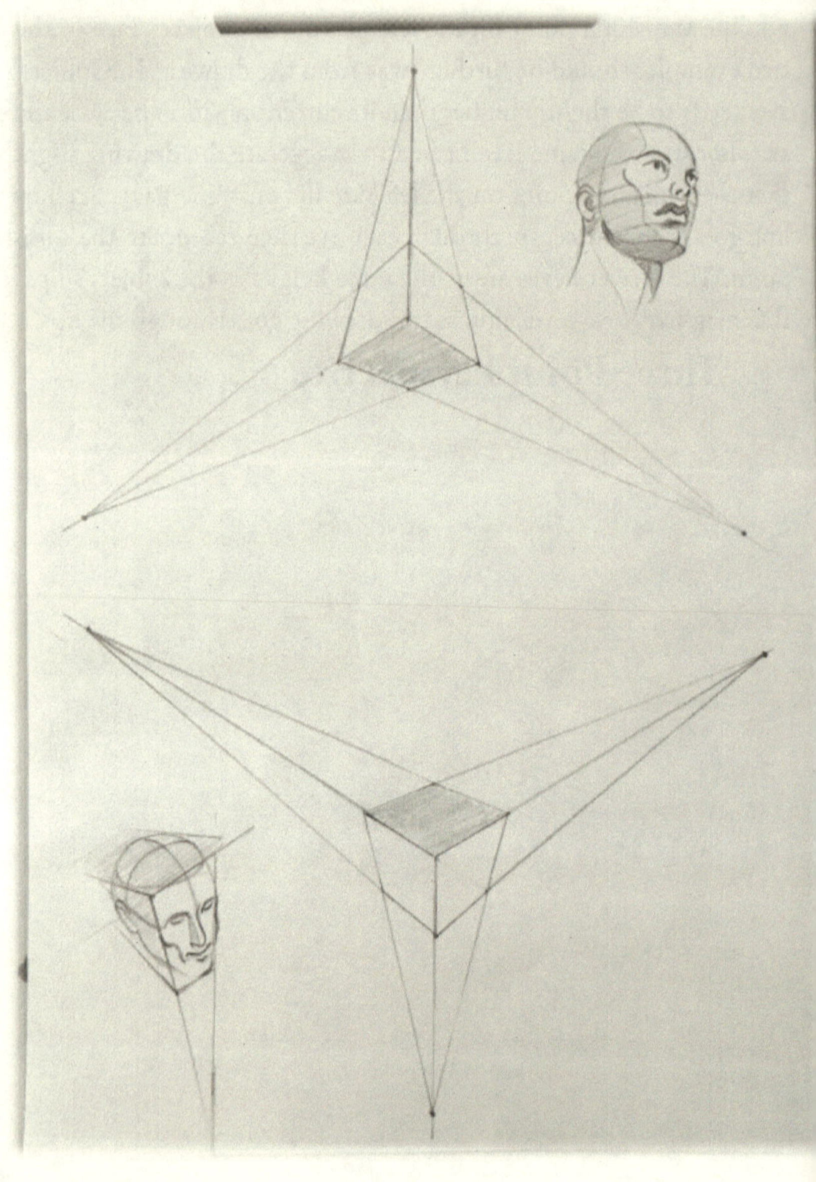

Three point perspective is only used when the subject is viewed from extreme angles. The third vanishing point is not on the line of the horizon but above or below it. Be mindful of three point perspective when you attempt to draw subjects from extreme angles.

Shedding light on some realities that are not usually discussed

Measuring

It is easy to make mistakes when you are using the pencil method outlined earlier for measuring angles and proportions. To avoid errors, make sure you straighten your elbow as much as you can and don't change your position. Do all your measurements and angles in one go without moving. If you move your chair or your stance slightly away from your original position, the rest of your measurements, angles and proportions will be inexact.

Bending and straightening your back during the measuring process will also make your drawing inaccurate. Make sure your back and elbow remain straight until you complete your measurements. With practice, this will become easier and more comfortable.

Sketch board

Make sure you choose the right sketch board as it is a key piece of your drawing equipment. If you plan to take your sketch board everywhere with you, choose a light one which is portable and easy to carry. Make sure it is not warped and has no bumps on it. When you attach a sheet of paper, make sure the edges of the paper are parallel to the edges of the sketch board. A good sketch board has a clip to secure the paper at the top, but you will also need clips on both sides of the board to keep the paper firmly in place.

Your sketch board should also be waterproof. This feature is essential only if you plan to sketch outdoors. Many boards warp over time if they are exposed to moisture.

There are two ways to use your sketch board: on an easel or holding it in one hand while drawing with the other. Whichever way you choose, you need to be in a comfortable position so that you can look directly at the sketch board. Your view needs to be perpendicular, not oblique. After years of sketching, some people realise that their way of looking at the sketch board is the main reason their drawings look odd. An oblique view leads to errors in perspective. Such errors cannot be fixed and those who try usually mess up another part of their drawing.

To avoid this basic mistake, always position yourself directly in front of your sketch board in a way that your view to the sketch board's surface is perpendicular. Make sure this becomes a habit before it is too late to change.

Amount of practice

It takes a huge amount of practice to develop good drawing skills. This simple fact is often overlooked. People who exercise great control over their pencil when drawing have spent countless hours practising. A tangible measure of your practice is the amount of paper you have used within a specific time period. Years ago, a dear friend and talented street artist told me that each time he finished his drawing practice, the entire floor of his room would be covered in paper. I still practise drawing lines and my drawing continues to improve. Sometimes I use a ream of A3 paper (approx. 5 kg) in a few days but then I realise i need even more practice as it takes years to master the skill of line drawing.

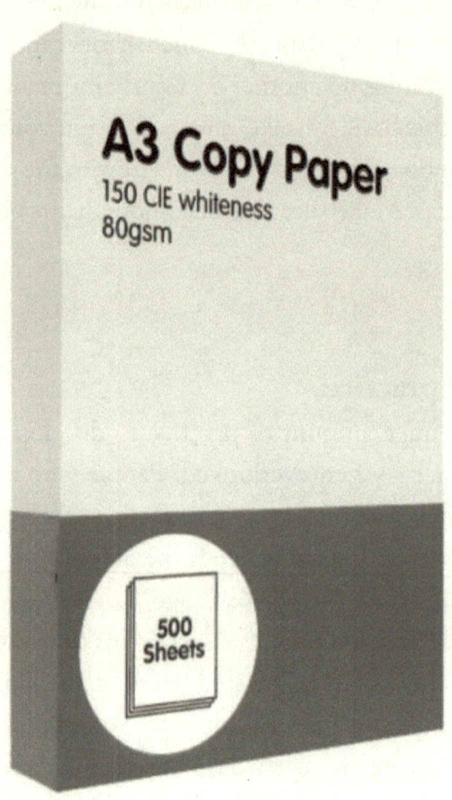

Some really important facts to know for people who draw portraits

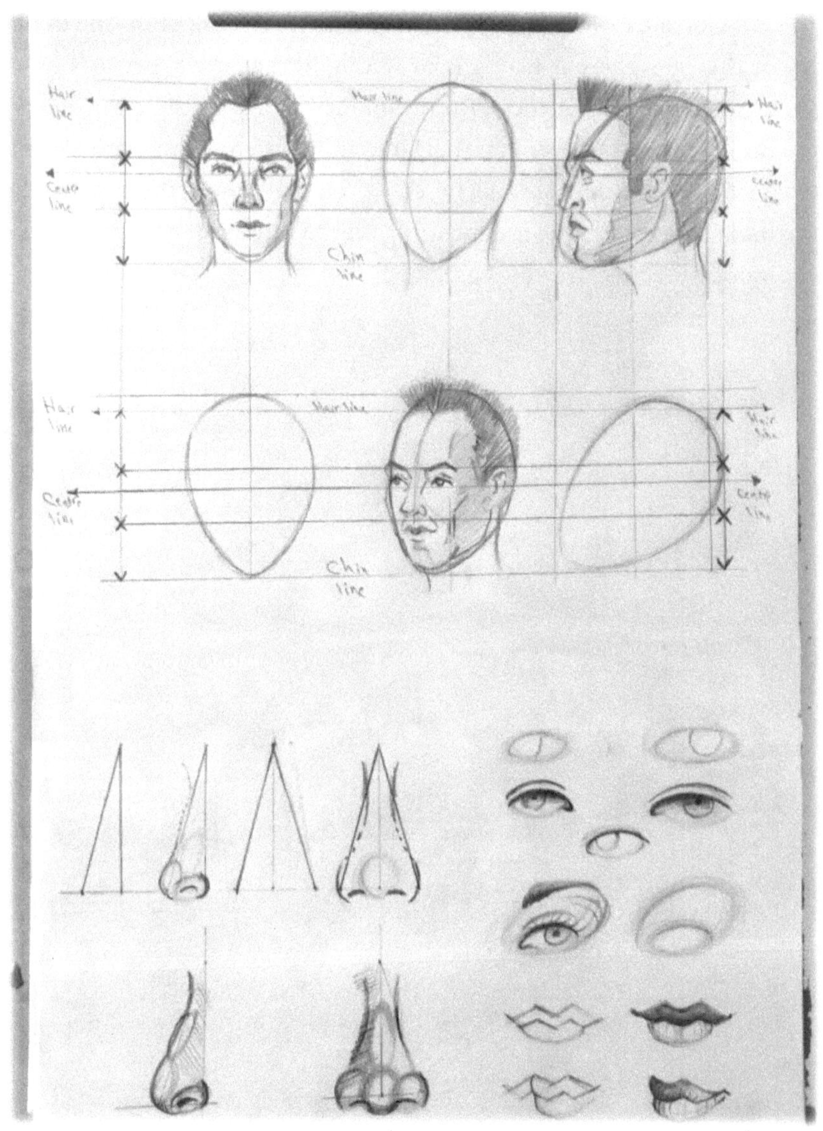
Hair line
Hair line
Hair line
Centre line
Centre line
Chin line
Hair line
Hair line
Hair line
Hair line
Centre line
Centre line
Chin line

Consider every head as an egg. Choose a hairline on the upper part of the egg. There is no right or wrong here as every person's hairline is different. Think of the bottom line of the egg as the chin line. Divide the distance between the hairline and the chin line into three equal parts and the rest should be easy. You can adjust these parts, making them shorter or longer depending on the forehead, nose and chin of the model. Practice drawing egg shapes

Notice how simple shapes can help you draw facial features. A great thing to remember is to draw a dark upper eye line. In quick sketches, you don't even have to draw a lower eye line unless the model has used eye liner. Draw a dark curved line on the upper part of an ellipse and see what you think. Usually the light source is above us, so the space just below the eye line is darker, whereas the upper part of the eyebrow and the lower lip are lighter.

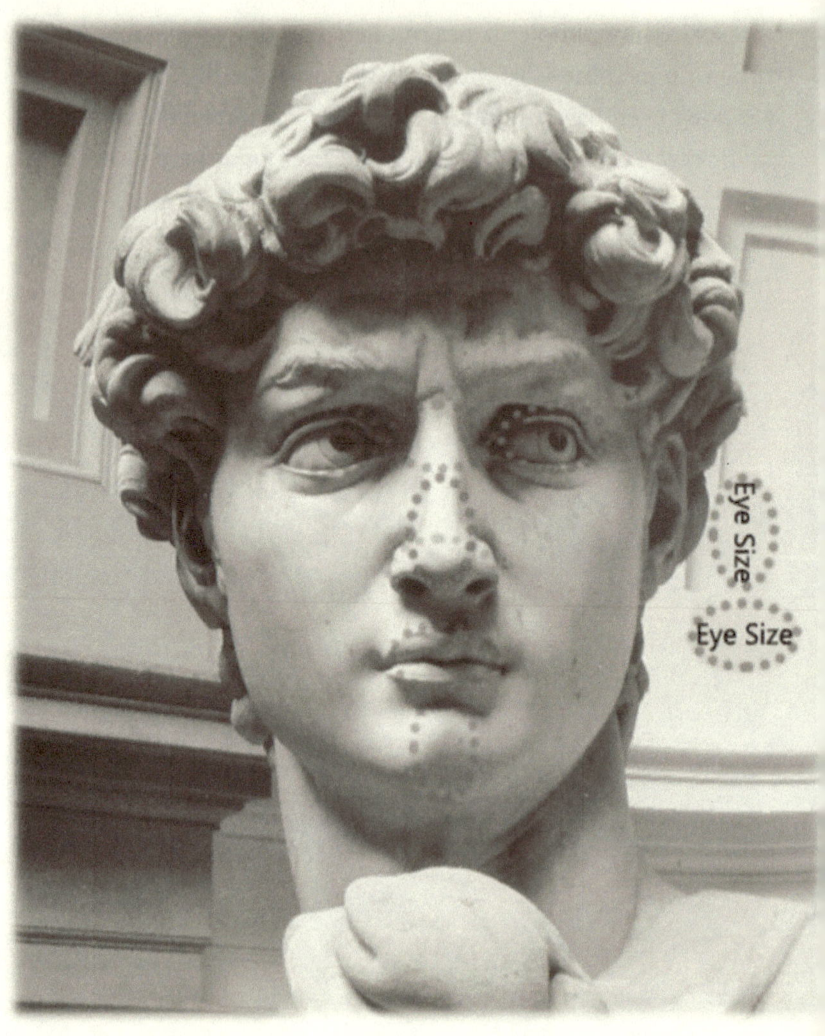

Draw smart

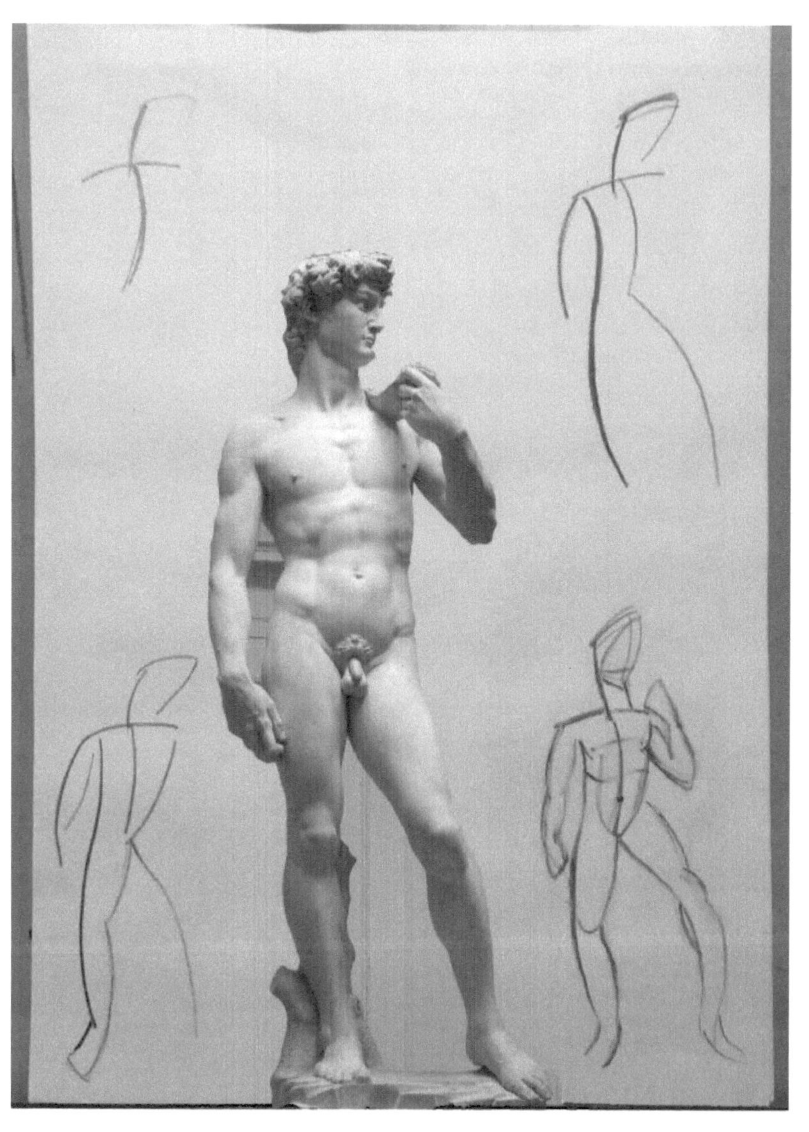

As a beginner, don't rush to complete your drawing. Take your time. Over time you will be able to draw more quickly. Initially you should focus on the basics, such as gesture lines. Feel free to use your creativity and exaggerate the lines but make sure you don't ruin the integral structure of the drawing. Exaggeration is one way to create a more attractive and dynamic drawing.

This is the smart way to draw. Take this advice and you will see that this is the smart way to increase your speed, little by little over time. Everything will improve, even your practice exercises, your stormy sketches. You can experiment with your stormy sketches. Slow them down and then speed them up again. Take five to ten minutes and then switch back to one to two minutes. Drawing smart helps you to avoid drawing unnecessary lines. Look at the sculpture of Michelangelo's David. See how his right leg forms a straight, strong line to show that his weight is on that leg. This is a basic feature, but it is very important in the drawing.

Realism versus Photorealism and Hyperrealism

With a few exceptions, most of the old masters created realistic drawings and paintings. Each one has a distinctive style which makes their work instantly recognisable. When we look at their brush strokes or the way they have created lines and shading, we see the individual variations that are like a key signature. Take Michelangelo for example. The sculptural quality of his paintings echoes the realism of his sculptures.

Although there are some similarities between the paintings of Michelangelo and Raphael, we would never mistake one for the other. Similarly, when we compare the works of Da Vinci, Rubens, Vermeer, Rembrandt and Goya, they are all unmistakable. They are similar only in that they all represent their subjects in a realistic way.

Let's look at another example: the work of Duccio, classified as Gothic art. Some might say that the work resembles a collage more than a realistic painting and appears more modern in style than of its time (14th Century). However, the subjects are recognisable and there is merit in the way the painter establishes the connections between them. In my opinion, the way Duccio painted the hands and facial features is quite revolutionary in Renaissance art. It is interesting how some modern artists continue to imitate the Gothic style and win prestigious prizes for their work.

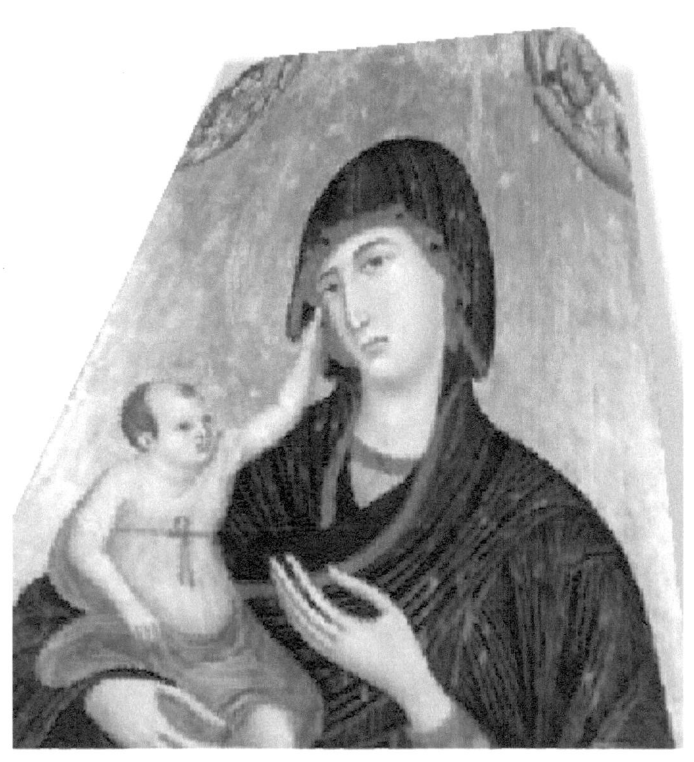

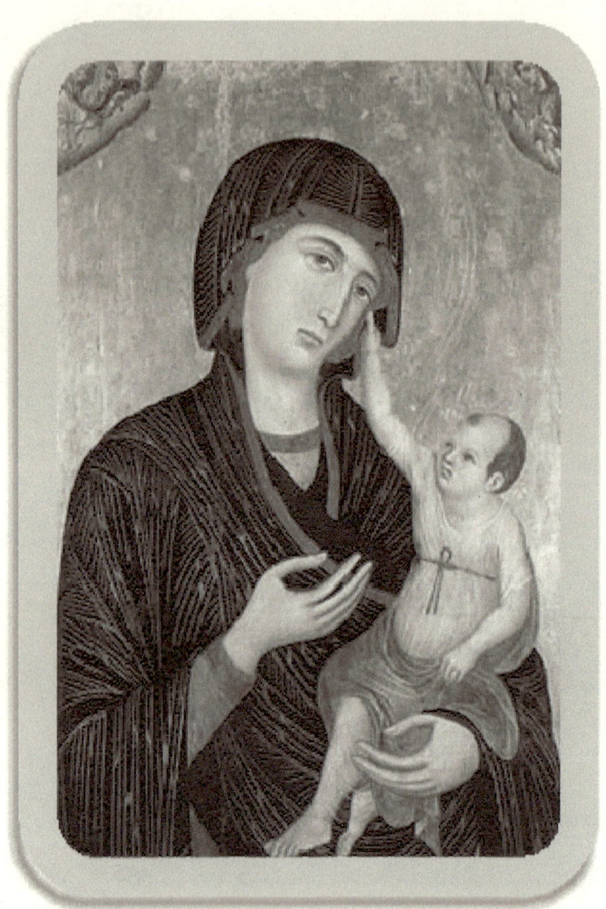

Although I admire all styles of art, I am not sure whether photorealism and hyperrealism can be considered as genuine art (In both of these styles, the artists try to create a photo-like darwing or painting. The only difference is that hyperrealism resembles a high-resolution photograph). When I compare different styles of drawing and painting, I can appreciate how the artists use their pencils and brushes in their own way to create their artworks. Once artists establish their own style it is there for us to admire in all their work. Regardless of the style of an artist's work, be it real, surreal, post-impressionist or abstract, there are always unique characteristics that make it easy to identify the creator.

I do not deny that a photorealist or a hyperrealist uses high-tech methods of colouring and shading to create pictures that are almost impossible to distinguish from actual photos. The problem is their works lack originality. We speculate on the method used to create the work, rather than on the work itself. It is impossible to identify the artist. Works by different artists look the same. Surely these artists need to develop their own unique style.

Why spend so much time creating these works when no one knows that you are the artist? No one can seek out your paintings or follow your progress. Such absolute uniformity of style does not seem to benefit the artists at all. We, as artists, should leave traces of ourselves in our work. I acknowledge that the artists who create works of photorealism and hyperrealism have extraordinary skills, but I feel there needs to be more constructive criticism to shed light on the negative aspects of this style.

A piece of art that can easily be attributed to its creator, will assist the artist to gain fans and followers much faster. It is a joy to be able to associate a piece to an artist instantly.

Why is art so important? There are three critical characteristics of real art that are often forgotten to the detriment of many art students. These characteristics are simplicity, greatness and aesthetics. Currently, many works designated as first-rate lack these qualities. When we look at a great work of art it attracts us, impresses us and touches us in some way. Some works affect us so deeply that we forget our everyday problems.

Great art can have a powerful effect on our lives. It can change the way we look at everything and greatly benefit our mental health. I hope this book will help you to appreciate art, create art, and make it a lifelong pursuit helping you to discover that your life, like your skills, will improve day by day.

Author's Note:

To my readers I say a sincere thank you for the time you have invested in reading this book. Please post a review if you believe that this book deserves to be read by more people. I would really appreciate your feedback. It will give me the courage and the motivation to write another book.

Sincerely,

Mahdi

www.ingramcontent.com/pod-product-compliance
Lightning Source LLC
LaVergne TN
LVHW091227150826
845673LV00003B/1046